A Gift for Diane

With Warm Thoughts
and Wishes
♡

From Lani
with Love

Published by American Greetings Corporation,
One American Road, Cleveland, Ohio 44144
Visit us at www.americangreetings.com

ISBN 1-4009-0871-X

Manufactured in China.

A Mother Is Love

A COLLECTION OF THOUGHTS
CELEBRATING MOTHERS

The fabric of family
is woven with threads
of laughter and tears,
pieces of dreams
and sharing...

...a patchwork
of stories
and memories
all held together
by a mother's
unconditional love.

All About Mothers

A mother's warm
and giving heart
blesses children from the start
With deep compassion
and concern,
expecting nothing in return.
A mother's tender,
busy hands
respond to little ones' demands,
Taking time
to teach and play
or gently hug each hurt away...

A mother's eyes
will always see
the goodness
in her family—
Her patience
and acceptance flow
as children strive
to learn and grow...

A mother's love
shines through the years,
to guide us
through life's doubts and fears
By making home
a haven of
contentment,
happiness, and love.

A mother
can add sunshine
to the dullest day
with just a smile,
erase a hurt
with a gentle kiss,
and set things right
with the briefest touch.
Her love
continually makes
this world
a happier place
to be.

Children
Do Not Realize

$\mathscr{A}$s children,

we can't comprehend

or fully realize

The meaning

of a mother's love—

how tender and how wise...

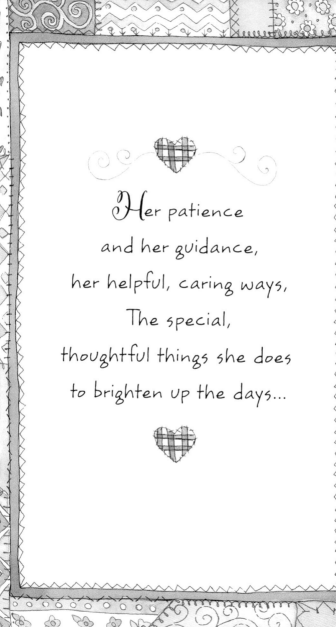

Her patience
and her guidance,
her helpful, caring ways,
The special,
thoughtful things she does
to brighten up the days...

But as we grow
we understand,
for we look back and see,
Through older eyes
and wiser hearts,
her love and loyalty...

*I*t's these

and many other things

that make her grow more dear

With every thought

and memory,

with every passing year.

Aren't Mothers
the Most Wonderful
People!

Aren't mothers
the most wonderful people!
It seems that
they're always on hand
To give you a boost
when you need it
And help you in something
you've planned...

Aren't mothers best friends
when you need them—
They prove it so often and well—
A mother's the one to confide in
'Cause you're positive
she'll never tell...

Aren't mothers
the most wonderful people!
The good points they have
are so many—
No wonder they're loved
and thought of so much—
And your own
is the nicest of any!

Mothers Know...

A little hug goes a long way.

Jelly jars make great vases.

Dandelions are beautiful.

There's no place like home.

Every drawing is a work of art.

Little voices have a lot to say
if you really listen.

Bedtime stories
stay in your heart forever.

Sometimes just one cookie
before dinner isn't all that bad.

Love is something
you never outgrow.

The Things That Matter Most

A mother always takes the time
to make your heart feel light,
With words like
"I'm so proud of you,"
or "Things will be all right..."

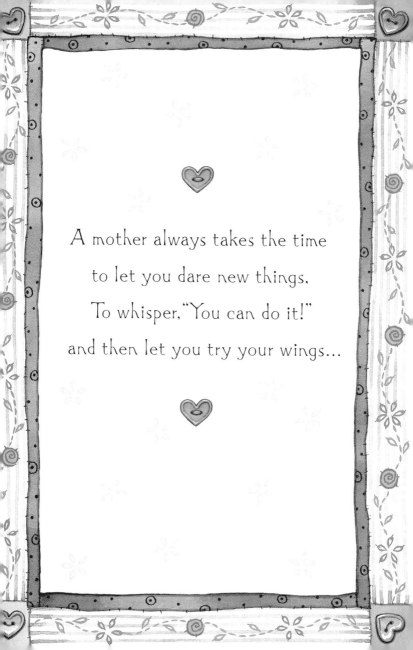

A mother always takes the time
to let you dare new things,
To whisper, "You can do it!"
and then let you try your wings...

A mother always takes the time
and goes to any length
To share her gifts
of truth and trust
and gentleness and strength...

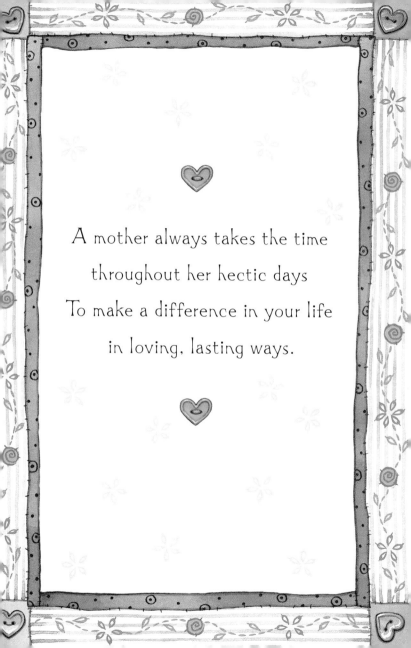

A mother always takes the time
throughout her hectic days
To make a difference in your life
in loving, lasting ways.

Mothers are angels
who lift us to our feet
when our own wings
have trouble
remembering
how to fly.

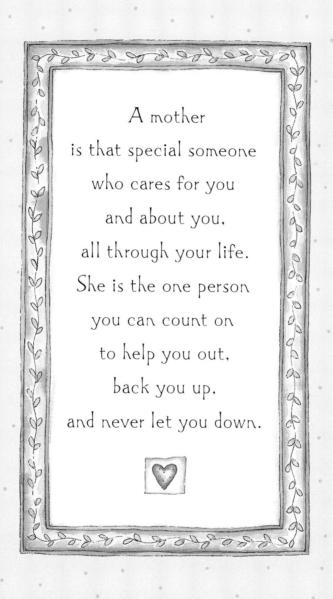

A mother
is that special someone
who cares for you
and about you,
all through your life.
She is the one person
you can count on
to help you out,
back you up,
and never let you down.

Real-life love
is what mothers
are all about.

Real-life love
is everyday moments
and favorite memories,
wise words
and lessons learned,
and hugs
when they're needed
the most...

It's giving support
when the going gets tough
and letting go
when children need
to be on their own.

It's laughter and tears,
listening from the heart,
and being there
for the ones she cares about—
always.

A Mother is...
the hand that always
reaches out to help,
the smile we look for
with each new success,
the eyes that see us
as we really are,
the heart
that only wants
our happiness.

A mother teaches
self-confidence
and the freedom
to be who we are,
to do what we can,
and to solve problems
the best
we know how...

A mother shows us
how to appreciate life
and to find happiness
in whatever
comes our way.
A mother holds us close
and lets us go,
all at the same time...

A mother is always there,
and always our best friend.

Mother...
She's the one
whose schedule
is the fullest,
whose days
are the busiest,
whose smiles
are the warmest...

...and whose place

in our lives

is the dearest.

Mother is

the heart

of home

and the joy

of all those

her love

has touched.

Mender of hearts,

Open and true,

Thoughtful and trustworthy,

Hug-giving, too,

Endlessly patient,

Ready with laughter...

Mothers are
treasures
Forever
and after.

Mothers sprinkle stardust on our dreams.

Caring more tenderly,

Sharing more generously,

Understanding more clearly,

Loving more dearly...

That's all part

of being a mother!

A mother is all things good—
patient smiles,
gentle hugs,
a warm and caring love—
the kind that
any child knows
is the most perfect love of all.

What Would We Do Without Mothers?

What would we do
without mothers?
How would the world survive?
Who would know how
to make rainy days fun
and who'd keep
the goldfish alive?

Where would we be
without mothers?
Who would believe
in our dreams?
Where could we turn
when we needed to hear
that nothing's as bad
as it seems?

How could we live
without mothers?
Who'd be our chauffeurs
and nurses?
And where in the world
could we put all the stuff
that mothers all keep
in their purses?

How would we learn

without mothers—

that we're loved

just the way that we are?

Who would applaud us

and say "don't give up"

and teach us

to reach for our star?

What would we do
without mothers?
Pretty much nothing,
I fear—
Because if we lived in a world
without mothers,
there wouldn't be anyone here!

$\mathcal{A}$ mother is

all the unforgettable memories

of your childhood—

the stories at bedtime,

comfort

during thunderstorms,

hot chocolate

on cold days...

$\mathcal{A}$ mother is

the patient understanding

that can deal with problems

big and small,

and when you're old enough

to be on your own,

she's a brave "good-bye"

and, always,

a warm "welcome home"...

$\mathcal{A}$ mother is

the warmth and security

you always remember,

the caring friendship

you someday grow into,

and all the memories

you never outgrow!

The value of
a wonderful mother
cannot be measured—

only treasured!